A BEACON BIOGRAPHY

Peyton
MANNING

Pete DiPrimio

PURPLE TOAD
PUBLISHING

Printing   1   2   3   4   5   6   7   8   9

A Beacon Biography

Big Time Rush
Carly Rae Jepsen
Drake
Harry Styles of One Direction
Jennifer Lawrence
Kevin Durant
Lorde
Markus "Notch" Persson, Creator of *Minecraft*
Neil deGrasse Tyson
Peyton Manning
Robert Griffin III (RG3)

Publisher's Cataloging-in-Publication Data
Pete DiPrimio.
  Peyton Manning / written by Pete DiPrimio.
    p. cm.
          Includes bibliographic references and index.
          ISBN 9781624690921
1. Manning, Peyton—Juvenile literature. 2. Football players—United States—Biography—Juvenile literature. I. Series: Beacon Biographies.
  GV939 2015
  796.332092

Library of Congress Control Number: 2014937125

eBook ISBN: 9781624690938

ABOUT THE AUTHOR: Pete DiPrimio is an award-winning Indiana sports writer and columnist, a long-time freelance writer with three published sports books pertaining to Indiana University, and a veteran children's author with nearly 20 published books. He's also a fitness instructor and has been a journalism adjunct lecturer.

PUBLISHER'S NOTE: The data in this book has been researched in depth, and to the best of our knowledge is factual. Although every measure is taken to give an accurate account, Purple Toad Publishing makes no warranty of the accuracy of the information and is not liable for damages caused by inaccuracies. This story has not been authorized or endorsed by Peyton Manning.

CONTENTS

Peyton Manning

It All Matters

"Omaha!" Peyton Manning shouted, and a nation heard. That happens when you're the NFL's most famous quarterback and microphones capture your mysterious football messages.

During the weeks leading to the 2014 Super Bowl, people across the country knew about "Omaha," not because it's one of Nebraska's largest cities, but because it was part of Manning's snap call before starting Denver's high-powered offense.

What does it mean?

Basically, it's a hurry-up-and-go call. Manning was telling the center to snap the ball.

Or was he?

"Omaha is a run play," Manning jokingly told *CBS Sports,* "but it could be a pass play or a play-action pass, depending on a couple things: which way we're going, the quarter, and the jerseys that we're wearing. It varies, really, from play to play. So, there's your answer to that one."

Manning could joke. Life was good again. He had overcome four neck surgeries that had ended his long career in Indianapolis and led to a new beginning in Denver. Many believed he was the greatest quarterback who ever lived—he had made 13 Pro Bowls, thrown for

No quarterback in the NFL runs the no-huddle offense, or reads defenses, better than Peyton Manning.

4,000 yards or more an NFL-record 13 times, won a record five NFL MVP Awards, and won one Super Bowl. Now he was about to prove his reputation once and for all.

During the 2013, season he'd set NFL records with 55 touchdown passes and 5,447 yards. He was, perhaps, the most famous athlete on the planet. He thrived with this simple yet effective approach: know what you're doing and get rid of the ball fast. If you do that, you won't get hit. If you don't get hit, you get to do it all over again. He prepared harder than anyone, studied more film, took more reps, and relentlessly went over little things that others overlooked.

Why?

Because it all mattered.

Manning was on top of the football mountain and no one could stop him—not even, it seemed, the Seattle Seahawks' league-best defense.

And yet . . .

Flash back to the summer of 2011.

Manning was playing catch in a private session, and it wasn't going well. His throws fluttered eight yards before hitting the turf. He couldn't lift a three-pound dumbbell. He couldn't push himself out of bed. Why? Because a herniated disc in his neck had damaged the nerve going to his right arm. After his surgeries, it seemed obvious: Manning was finished.

Not to him.

Those neck surgeries had left Manning's career in doubt. He'd been a superstar for the Indianapolis Colts, setting passing records on the field when he wasn't earning off-the-field praise for his funny TV commercials and even funnier guest appearances on *Saturday Night Live*.

Now, nothing was sure except Manning would miss the 2011 season opener, and then the first month, and then, finally, the whole season.

Stories spread about how hard Manning was struggling—but many weren't true.

"I certainly had my concerns that entire time," Manning said during a Super Bowl media session. "Doctors couldn't tell me anything definite. When doctors can't tell you, how do you know?

"There was a lot of narrative out there on what I couldn't do. How did they know? I was throwing in private the entire time. There was a lot of misinformation."

With Manning as their quarterback, the Colts had been one of the NFL's best teams for a decade. Without him, they crashed to a 2-14 record. That got them the NFL's No. 1 draft pick, and they took Stanford's Andrew Luck. Team officials saw the talented Luck as the new Peyton Manning.

So what do you do with the old Manning? Manning wanted to stay in Indianapolis, but was that best for him and the Colts? After a lot of thought, owner Jim Irsay cut him from the team. The Colts would start over. So would Manning. But where?

Manning picked Denver and signed a five-year, $96 million contract in the spring of 2012. Excitement grew in the Mile High City, but still, at 35 years old with a surgically repaired neck, nothing was sure except one thing:

Manning was determined to come back better than ever.

The Manning home in New Orleans where Peyton grew up.

Growing Up, Getting Crazy

Peyton Williams Manning was born on March 24, 1976, in New Orleans. His first name came from his sports-loving uncle Peyton, a cotton and soybean farmer from Mississippi. Little Peyton grew up in the city's historic Garden District hating to lose, in part because his family was so good at winning. His father, Archie, had been an All-American quarterback at the University of Mississippi and then a standout player for the NFL's New Orleans Saints. His mother, Olivia, had been Mississippi's homecoming queen. Older brother Cooper was a promising football wide receiver. He might have been a pro if a spinal cord problem hadn't ended his career after he'd earned a scholarship to Mississippi. Younger brother Eli became an All-American quarterback at Mississippi, then went on to win two Super Bowls with the New York Giants.

As a boy, Peyton's competitiveness sometimes got him into trouble. He got angry when people made mistakes, and he wasn't shy about blaming them. It got so bad his father decided he wouldn't coach him anymore in youth sports.

When Peyton was twelve, he played on a youth basketball team. After a loss, the coach told them they lost because they weren't ready

Peyton's parents, Archie and Olivia, and older brother Cooper, helped keep Peyton grounded as he grew up. Archie was a successful college and NFL quarterback.

to play. Peyton told him they lost because "You don't know what you're doing."

That night Archie drove Peyton to the coach's house and made him apologize.

Peyton had grown out of his bad attitude by the time he got to New Orleans' Isidore Newman High School. In his three years as the starting quarterback, Isidore Newman went 34-5. He threw for 7,207 yards and 92 touchdowns (a lot of his passes his first two years went to Cooper). As a senior, Peyton was named the Gatorade Circle of Champions National Player of the Year.

Every major college program in the country wanted him. That included Mississippi, where his father had gone. Eventually, Peyton decided he wanted to make his own mark somewhere else, and no coach made a bigger impression on him than Tennessee offensive coordinator David Cutcliffe. Peyton would become a Volunteer.

Another big moment soon followed, although he didn't know it. The summer before arriving at Tennessee, he met a smart girl,

Ashley Thompson. They began dating. On St. Patrick's Day in 2001, they got married.

Peyton was popular when he got to Tennessee, but things got wild when, as a sophomore, he led the Volunteers to their first win over powerhouse Alabama in ten years. Soon, people began naming their babies—boys and girls—after him. Twins from Knoxville were named Peyton and Manning. Parents would bring their babies to Tennessee practices, wanting to take photos with Peyton. He asked his father for advice. Archie had none to give.

"I only had dogs and cats named after me," Archie said.

Peyton became the starter five games into his freshman season of 1994 when veteran Todd Helton suffered a season-ending knee injury. Peyton made national news when he threw for three touchdowns against South Carolina. He was 7-1 as the Volunteers starter and was named SEC Freshman of the Year.

Peyton and Tennessee coach Phillip Fulmer won a lot of games together, but could never win that elusive national championship.

Peyton was a successful college quarterback in 1996, and younger brother Eli wanted to know all about it. Eli went on to his own college and NFL success, winning a pair of Super Bowls with the New York Giants.

His first 300-yard passing game came against Georgia as a sophomore. Tennessee went 11-1 and only a loss to Florida prevented the team from winning the national championship. Peyton threw just four interceptions in 380 attempts to set an NCAA record for lowest interception percentage (1.05 percent). That wasn't a fluke. By the time he finished his college career, he'd thrown just 33 interceptions in 1,381 pass attempts, another NCAA interception percentage record (2.39 percent).

Peyton led the Volunteers to a 10-2 record as a junior while becoming the first Tennessee quarterback to throw for more than 3,000 yards in a season (3,287). He graduated after his junior season. Many thought he would leave to enter the NFL draft. Instead, he stayed for his senior season and threw for 3,819 yards and 37 touchdowns while leading the Volunteers to the SEC championship and an 11-2 record. Tennessee was 39-6 with Peyton as the starter.

He was the Heisman Trophy runner-up to Michigan defensive back Charles Woodson and won the Davey O'Brien and Johnny Unitas awards as the nation's best quarterback. He also won the Sullivan Award, which goes to the nation's top amateur athlete based on leadership, character, and athletic ability. He was named Academic All-American. He set 42 NCAA, SEC, and Tennessee records. He threw for 11,201 yards and 89 touchdowns. That included a 400-yard passing game against Florida and a 500-yard passing game against Kentucky.

Peyton was also successful in the classroom, just as much for his hard work as his intelligence. His SAT score entering Tennessee was barely above average at 1030 (on the 1600 scale then being used), but he graduated from the university's College of Communication and Information with the year's highest GPA.

It all mattered, you see.

Studying for his college classes was just as important to Peyton Manning as football.

Peyton Manning and the Indianapolis Colts were a perfect fit. He set records, earned MVP honors and won a Super Bowl during his time there.

The Colts Years

The Indianapolis Colts had the NFL's No. 1 draft pick in 1998. They were going to take a quarterback and there were only two real choices—Peyton Manning and Washington State's Ryan Leaf.

Leaf had the stronger arm, but far less prime-time experience. He'd only had one really big year at Washington State, when as a junior he threw for 33 touchdown passes and led Washington State to the Rose Bowl. He gave up his final college season to enter the NFL Draft and arrived at the NFL Combine—a multi-day camp in Indianapolis where teams evaluate prospects—overweight. Manning showed up in shape and football wise beyond his years. The Colts picked Manning. San Diego took Leaf, who in a couple of years was out of the NFL because of injuries, personal problems, and bad behavior.

Indianapolis quickly realized it had a special quarterback, as much for his smart play as his accurate arm. Manning quickly memorized the Colts' entire playbook.

During Manning's rookie season, the Colts began using a no-huddle offense called "Lightning" whenever they fell behind. That meant Manning, rather than coaches, would call the plays. Because

The Colts made Peyton the No. 1 pick in the 1998 NFL draft, and boy did it pay off.

there was no huddle, defenses didn't have time to substitute players. Manning could wear them out and keep them off balance.

And so he did. Manning got so good at it, and he studied so much film on opposing defenses, that he knew what they were going to do no matter how well they disguised it. After a couple of years, the Colts used "Lightning" all the time.

Peyton wasn't perfect as a rookie. He threw an NFL-worst 28 interceptions. But he also threw for 26 touchdowns and 3,739 yards. The Colts went just 3-13, mostly because of bad defense.

That quickly changed. The next year Indianapolis went 13-3 and made the playoffs. The Colts won at least 10 games for nine straight years. They won the 2007 Super Bowl when Peyton was named the MVP after throwing for 247 yards and a touchdown in a 29-17 win over Chicago.

In 2003, Manning won his first NFL MVP Award, sharing it with Tennessee quarterback Steve McNair. He also won it in 2004, 2008, and 2009 with the Colts.

In 2009, Indianapolis won its first 14 games. With the NFL's best record clinched, coaches rested most of the starters in the second half of the fifteenth game against the New York Jets. They said they wanted the team to be healthy for the playoffs. Fans booed because no team had gone unbeaten since the 1972 Miami Dolphins, and no team had ever finished 19-0. The Colts lost that game and then the next one before going on to the Super Bowl, where they lost to the New Orleans Saints. Manning's late interception clinched the Saints' 31-17 victory.

Still, everybody respected Peyton Manning. New England quarterback Tom Brady, a three-time Super Bowl winner and also one of the best to ever play, said Manning "set the standard" for quarterbacks.

"To me, he's the greatest of all time. He's a friend, and someone I always watch and admire, because he always wants to improve, he always wants to get better, and he doesn't settle for anything less than the best."

Injury demanded that the best take a rest. In May 2011, Peyton had neck surgery to take care of neck pain and arm weakness that had bothered him the previous few seasons. It didn't work and he eventually had another surgery—cervical fusion, which joined the bones in his neck together—that fall. That meant his NFL-record 208 starts to begin a career was over. He missed the entire season.

In November, he moved in with his old college offensive coordinator, David Cutcliffe, now the head coach at Duke. Manning had to relearn how to throw a football.

"I didn't know where I was headed," Manning told *Sports Illustrated*. "I didn't know if I'd be able to perform again."

He thought about giving up. Ashley wouldn't let him. *Try*, she said.

And so he did.

Manning bobble-head

After the Colts cut Manning because of his neck injury, he signed with the Denver Broncos with a big goal: win at least one more Super Bowl.

Chapter 4

Super Disappointment

Manning had to smile. Seattle cornerback Richard Sherman had said Manning threw "ducks." In other words, his passes were slow and wobbled through the air. Manning agreed—to a point.

"They say [Sherman is] a smart player, and I don't think that's a real reach what he's saying there," Manning said during a pre-game interview. "I do throw ducks. I've thrown a lot of yards and touchdown ducks, so I'm actually quite proud of it."

Later, when excitement for the 2014 Super Bowl was building in the days before the game, Sherman joined the pregame chatter. He knew how good Manning was.

"He's a great quarterback," Sherman said. "He does a great job. He throws an accurate ball. He gets it on time."

Manning was ready for a big game. In 2012, his first season with Denver, he won the NFL's Comeback Player of the Year award by throwing for 4,659 yards and 37 touchdowns. He was even better in his record-breaking second season. No team had stopped him or the Denver offense, which had set a record by averaging 37.9 points. Yes, Seattle had the NFL's best defense, but Manning was ready. No quarterback had prepared longer and harder.

The game was played at New Jersey's $1.6 billion MetLife Stadium. Usually NFL officials chose warm-weather sites, but this time they gambled on the weather, and got lucky. The temperature was 49 degrees at kickoff. Hours after the game, a major snowstorm hit the area.

By then Manning and Denver had been hit by another storm.

Manning and the Broncos wanted to make an early Super Bowl statement, and they did—but in a bad way. On the first play, center Manny Ramirez's bad snap flew past a surprised Manning, who was still calling the signals. The ball bounced into the end zone and wound up a safety. Twelve seconds into the game, Seattle led 2-0, the fastest score in Super Bowl history.

"It was a crazy start," Manning said. "Not the way you expect to start the game."

It quickly got worse. By halftime, Denver trailed 22-0. Seattle's defense hit hard and often. The Broncos' five offensive linemen couldn't block the Seahawks' four defensive linemen. Peyton had little time to throw and when he did, big Seahawks were in his face.

The Broncos' goal to start the second half was simple—stop Seattle on its first possession, score a touchdown, and they'd have a chance.

It didn't work out. Seattle's Percy Harvin returned the second half kickoff for a touchdown. That made it 29-0. A few minutes later, it was 36-0.

Pride was all Manning and the Broncos had left in the 43-8 defeat.

Manning set a Super Bowl record with 34 completions, but most of them were short passes that barely dented Seattle's defense. He threw for 280 yards, about 70 below his average. He managed just one touchdown—a 14-yard pass to Demaryius Thomas at the end of the third quarter—while throwing two interceptions. Seattle linebacker Malcolm Smith returned one of the interceptions 69 yards for a touchdown and was named Super Bowl MVP. Peyton was sacked for the first time in the playoffs, fumbled, and had, by far, his worst day as a Bronco.

"I'm disappointed for our entire team," Manning said. "We worked hard to get to this point. Overcame a lot of obstacles. Put in a lot of hard work just to have this opportunity. But to finish this way, it certainly is disappointing. It's a bitter pill to swallow."

It was not, he added, an embarrassment, although others disagreed.

Denver and its general manager, John Elway, were used to upsetting Super Bowls. Elway was the quarterback when the Broncos lost 39-20, 42-10, and 55-10 in Super Bowls before finally winning their last two. Elway had taken over Denver in 2011, and was huge in convincing Manning to join the Broncos. They would work hard to come back, Elway said. Manning said they would use the loss as motivation to be better the next year.

Afterward, Seattle's Sherman tweeted this about Manning: "Peyton is the Classiest person/player I have ever met! I could learn so much from him! Thank you for being a great Competitor and person."

Seattle cornerback Richard Sherman got in the last word with Manning after Seattle beat Denver in the 2014 Super Bowl.

Peyton often represents the NFL in reaching out to fans. That includes sailors aboard the Navy's Nimitz-class aircraft carrier USS John C. Stennis.

Beyond Football

Retire?

Are you kidding?

Manning wasn't about to quit football after the 2014 Super Bowl.

"I still enjoy playing football," he said during a Super Bowl press conference. "I feel a little better than I thought I would at this point coming off that surgery. I still enjoy the preparation part of it, that work part of it. . . .

"I think as soon as I stop enjoying it, and I can't produce, and I can't help the team, that's when I'll stop playing."

Manning didn't disappear after the Super Bowl loss. Five days later he was on the California coast playing golf at Pebble Beach, one of the world's great courses, as part of the AT&T Pebble Beach National Pro-Am. The event helps raise money for Northern California charities.

"It's too hard to beat being out here, one of the Lord's great creations," Manning said in a press conference. "Great tournament, great cause—glad to get invited to play."

Pro golfer Phil Mickelson was happy Peyton was invited.

"He's a huge asset to this tournament, brings a lot to this event and what it's about," Mickelson told ESPN.com. "He helps bring [the] game of golf to other people who wouldn't be exposed to the game."

Peyton has always helped people. When Hurricane Katrina damaged much of his hometown of New Orleans in 2005, he and Eli volunteered to help. That included delivering 30,000 pounds of water, Gatorade, baby formula, diapers, and pillows.

Even after signing with Denver, Peyton remained committed to Peyton Manning Children's Hospital at St. Vincent in Indianapolis. In 2007, he and Ashley made a big donation to the hospital to help children. Children have always been special to them. In April 2011 they had twins—a boy, Marshall, and a girl, Mosley.

Countless children have been helped at Indianapolis' Peyton Manning Children's Hospital, and it goes beyond medical care. Here a young patient gets serenaded by Sgt. Jeremy Otkin (near left), Sgt. Jay Goldsborough (in the back) and Spc. Lee Stephen (right) of the 82nd Airborne Division Chorus.

Peyton and Ashley also started the PeyBack Foundation, which has given more than $5 million in grants over the years to organizations for underprivileged children in Colorado, Indiana, Tennessee, and Louisiana. The foundation also passes out 800 bags of groceries each year for Thanksgiving in Denver and Indianapolis.

He and his family—Archie, Eli, and Cooper—run the five-day Manning Passing Academy. He and Archie wrote a book in 2000, *Manning: A Father, His Sons, and a Football Legacy.* In 2009, he, Archie, and Eli wrote a children's book, *Family Huddle,* about how the Manning brothers grew up playing football.

By the end of 2013, Peyton and Eli had competed against each other three times in the NFL. The media called it the Manning Bowl. Peyton was 3-0 against Eli, winning 26-21 and 38-14 while with the Colts, and 41-23 while with the Broncos.

Peyton and his wife Ashley use the organization they started, the Peyback Foundation, to help underprivileged children.

Besides Manning's many commercials (including DIRECTV, Papa John's, Wheaties cereal, Reebok, MasterCard, Buick, Gatorade, and ESPN's *SportsCenter*), and *Saturday Night Live* appearances, he was also a guest voice along with Eli and Cooper in a 2009 episode of the TV cartoon *The Simpsons*.

In 2013, Peyton made $12 million in endorsements and $18 million with the Broncos. That income ranked fifth among NFL players.

Some said people would remember Peyton for his two Super Bowl failures. Not true, said journalism professor Laurie Lattimore-Volkmann, a mother of two boys who were huge Peyton fans.

In an open letter that ran in the *San Jose Mercury News*, Lattimore-Volkmann wrote, "[T]his mom of two young boys believes your legacy has never been stronger. Whether you win another game, your accomplishments in football are nothing short of

Nobody in NFL history has thrown more touchdown passes than Peyton. On this play on October 19, 2014, he broke Bret Favre's record by throwing his 509th career touchdown.

Of all the important moments in Peyton's career, one of the most special was when the University of Tennessee retired his jersey.

remarkable. . . . But it's your character that sets you apart. That's a legacy that matters."

Peyton gets a lot of fan mail and answers much of it, especially mail from people who are hurting through injury or illness or tragedy. Sometimes he calls them while he drives home after practice.

On that Super Bowl-losing night in February 2014, after perhaps the worst game of his professional career, what some called a nationally televised embarrassment, when most players couldn't have left New Jersey soon enough, Peyton stayed to sign autographs. He made his fans feel special.

It all matters, you see.

Passing

Year	Team	G	At	Comp	Pct	Att/G	Yds	Avg	Yds/G	TD	Int	Rate
2014	Denver Broncos	10	407	273	67.1	40.7	3,301	8.1	330.1	30	9	107.1
2013	Denver Broncos	16	659	450	68.3	41.2	5,477	8.3	342.3	55	10	115.1
2012	Denver Broncos	16	583	400	68.6	36.4	4,659	8.0	291.2	37	11	105.8
2011	Indianapolis Colts	0	--	--	--	0.0	--	--	--	--	0.0	0.0
2010	Indianapolis Colts	16	679	450	66.3	42.4	4,700	6.9	293.8	33	17	91.9
2009	Indianapolis Colts	16	571	393	68.8	35.7	4,500	7.9	281.2	33	16	99.9
2008	Indianapolis Colts	16	555	371	66.8	34.7	4,002	7.2	250.1	27	12	95.0
2007	Indianapolis Colts	16	515	337	65.4	32.2	4,040	7.8	252.5	31	14	98.0
2006	Indianapolis Colts	16	557	362	65.0	34.8	4,397	7.9	274.8	31	9	101.0
2005	Indianapolis Colts	16	453	305	67.3	28.3	3,747	8.3	234.2	28	10	104.1
2004	Indianapolis Colts	16	497	336	67.6	31.1	4,557	9.2	284.8	49	10	121.1
2003	Indianapolis Colts	16	566	379	67.0	35.4	4,267	7.5	266.7	29	10	99.0
2002	Indianapolis Colts	16	591	392	66.3	36.9	4,200	7.1	262.5	27	19	88.8
2001	Indianapolis Colts	16	547	343	62.7	34.2	4,131	7.6	258.2	26	23	84.1
2000	Indianapolis Colts	16	571	357	62.5	35.7	4,413	7.7	275.8	33	15	94.7
1999	Indianapolis Colts	16	533	331	62.1	33.3	4,135	7.8	258.4	26	15	90.7
1998	Indianapolis Colts	16	575	326	56.7	35.9	3,739	6.5	233.7	26	28	71.2
TOTAL		250	8,859	5,805	65.5	35.4	68,265	7.7	273.1	521	228	97.7

Rushing

Year	Team	G	Att	Att/G	Yds	Avg	Yds/G	TD	Lng	1st
2014	Denver Broncos	10	14	1.4	-6	-0.4	-0.6	0	4	0
2013	Denver Broncos	16	32	2	-31	-1	-1.9	1	1T	1
2012	Denver Broncos	16	23	1.4	6	0.3	0.4	0	10	2
2011	Indianapolis Colts	0	--	0	--	--	--	--	--	--
2010	Indianapolis Colts	16	18	1.1	18	1	1.1	0	27	2
2009	Indianapolis Colts	16	19	1.2	-13	-0.7	-0.8	0	3	0
2008	Indianapolis Colts	16	20	1.2	21	1.1	1.3	1	12	4
2007	Indianapolis Colts	16	20	1.2	-5	-0.3	-0.3	3	4	4
2006	Indianapolis Colts	16	23	1.4	36	1.6	2.2	4	12	7
2005	Indianapolis Colts	16	33	2.1	45	1.4	2.8	0	12	6
2004	Indianapolis Colts	16	25	1.6	38	1.5	2.4	0	19	4
2003	Indianapolis Colts	16	28	1.8	26	0.9	1.6	0	10	3
2002	Indianapolis Colts	16	38	2.4	148	3.9	9.2	2	13	11
2001	Indianapolis Colts	16	35	2.2	157	4.5	9.8	4	33T	9
2000	Indianapolis Colts	16	37	2.3	116	3.1	7.2	1	14	10
1999	Indianapolis Colts	16	35	2.2	73	2.1	4.6	2	13	8
1998	Indianapolis Colts	16	15	0.9	62	4.1	3.9	0	15	5
TOTAL		250	415	1.7	691	1.7	2.8	18	33	76

1976   Peyton Williams Manning is born on March 24, in New Orleans.

1994   He graduates from Isidore Newman High School and becomes a Volunteer at the University of Tennessee. He is named SEC freshman of the year.

1997   He graduates from UT's College of Communication and Information at the top of his class.

1998   He is chosen by the Indiana Colts as the No. 1 NFL Draft Pick.

1999   Peyton and his girlfriend, Ashley Thompson, start the PeyBack Foundation, a charity that supports programs for kids at risk. Peyton begins visiting children at St. Vincent Hospital in Indianapolis.

2000   Peyton publishes a book with his father, Archie, called *Manning: A Father, His Sons, and a Football Legacy.*

2001   Peyton and Ashley marry on March 17.

2003   Peyton receives his first NFL MVP Award. He will be chosen again in 2004, 2008, and 2009.

2007   The Colts win the Super Bowl 29-17 over Chicago; Manning is named the Super Bowl MVP. He and Ashley make a sizable donation to sponsor the Peyton Manning Children's Hospital at St. Vincent in Indianapolis.

2009   The Colts make it to another Super Bowl, but the New Orleans Saints beat them 31-17. Peyton publishes a children's book, *Family Huddle,* with Archie and Eli.

2011   Peyton suffers a herniated disc and misses the entire season. Twins Marshall and Mosley are born in April.

2012   Peyton signs a five-year, $96 million contract with the Denver Broncos.

2013   His 55 touchdown passes and 5,447 yards for the season help the Broncos reach the Super Bowl. He is again chosen as the NFL MVP.

2014   Super Bowl XLVIII is a disappointment for the Broncos, who lose 43-8 to the Seattle Seahawks; Manning sees it as a motivation to do better the next year.

Books

The Denver Post. *Peyton Manning: Leader of the Broncos.* Chicago: Triumph Books, 2013.

Inspirational Stories. *Peyton Manning: The Inspirational Story of Football Superstar Peyton Manning.* Kindle Edition, 2013.

Kiszla, Mark. *No Plan B: Peyton Manning's Comeback with the Denver Broncos.* Lanham, MD: Taylor Trade Publishing, 2013.

Manning, Peyton, and Archie, with John Underwood. *Manning.* New York: Harper Entertainment, 2000.

Manning, Peyton, Eli, and Archie, with Jim Madsen. *Family Huddle.* New York: Scholastic Press, 2009.

Works Consulted

Associated Press. "Manning had concerns about his comeback." January 29, 2014. http://www.heraldtimesonline. com/sports/manning-had-concerns-about-his-comeback/article_e0c645ca-6075-523b-9e54-d2931294b246. html

Chappell, Mike. "Peyton Manning." *Indianapolis Star,* May 4, 2012.

Chattanoogan.com. "University of Tennessee 2013 Peyton Manning Scholarship Awarded." *The Chattanoogan,* June 19, 2013.

Corbett, Jim. "Gone in 40 seconds: Peyton Manning's presnap routine." *USA Today,* September 13, 2006.

Corbett, Jim. "Reflective Peyton Manning enjoying 'uncle time' with Eli's new daughter." *USA Today,* January 29, 2014.

Hanzus, Dan. "Peyton Manning: 'I certainly want to keep playing.'" NFL.com, January 26, 2014. http://www.nfl. com/news/story/0ap2000000318039/article/peyton-manning-i-certainly-want-to-keep-playing

Hayes, Reggie. "Could Super Bowl be Manning's farewell?" *The Fort Wayne News-Sentinel,* January 25, 2014. http://www.news-sentinel.com/apps/pbcs.dll/article?AID=/20140125/SPORTS/140129738/-1/ajaxnewslist

Jenkins, Lee. "Denver Broncos' Peyton Manning named SI's Sportsman of the Year." *Sports Illustrated,* December 15, 2013.

Kay, Alex. "Examining Peyton Manning's Omaha Craze heading into 2014 Super Bowl." *Bleacher Report,* February 2, 2014. http://bleacherreport.com/articles/1945376-examining-peyton-mannings-omaha-craze-heading-into-2014-super-bowl

Klis, Mike. "Broncos, Peyton Manning struggle in Super Bowl Blowout by Seahawks." *The Denver Post,* February 2, 2014. http://www.denverpost.com/broncos/ci_25048459/broncos-peyton-manning-super-bowl-blowout-seahawks

Lattimore-Volkmann. "Dear Peyton Manning: An open letter from a mom." *San Jose Mercury News,* February 6, 2014. http://www.mercurynews.com/sports/ci_25092563/peyton-manning-open-letter-mom

Legwold, Jeff. "Peyton Manning: 'I do throw ducks.'" ESPN.com, January 31, 2014. http://espn.go.com/new-york/nfl/story/_/id/10376275/super-bowl-peyton-manning-denver-broncos-says-throws-touchdown-ducks

Lupica, Mike. "Peyton Manning proves doubters wrong with Super Bowl appearance." *New York Daily News,* January 29, 2014. http://www.nydailynews.com/sports/football/lupica-legacy-super-mann-polian-call-critics-ludicrous-article-1.1594918

Mandell, Nina. "Peyton Manning did not want a pep talk from the Governor of Washington." *USA Today,* February 2014. http://ftw.usatoday.com/2014/02/washington-governor-tried-to-give-peyton-manning-a-pep-talk-after-super-bowl-loss/

Peyton Manning Plays Pebble Beach Pro-AM. http://espn.go.com/nfl/story/_/id/10422657/peyton-manning-denver-broncos-gets-back-horse-pebble-beach-pro-am

Peyton Manning University of Tennessee Biography. http://www.utsports.com/sports/m-footbl/mtt/peyton_manning_834172.html

Prunty, Brendan. "Super Bowl 2014: How Seahawks defense discovered and exploited Peyton Manning's tell." *The Star-Ledger,* February 2, 2014. http://www.nj.com/super-bowl/index.ssf/2014/02/super_bowl_2014_seahawks_defense.html

Rooney, Jennifer. "Best and Worst Peyton Manning Ads of All Time." *Forbes,* January 29, 2014. http://www.forbes.com/sites/jenniferrooney/2014/01/29/best-and-worst-peyton-manning-ads-of-all-time/

Soto, Lindsay. "Tom Brady quote on Peyton Manning for Top Players of 2011 Reactions." NFL Network, July 3, 2014. http://blogs.nfl.com/2011/07/03/the-top-100-comes-down-to-brady-manning/?module=HP_headlines

Wetzel, Dan. "Peyton Manning leaves crushing Super Bowl loss with reputation intact." *Yahoo Sports*, February 2, 2014. http://sports.yahoo.com/news/peyton-manning-leaves-crushing-super-bowl-loss-with-reputation-intact-065205260.html

Zaas, Stuart. "Peyton Manning Named Associated Press Comeback Player of the Year." DenverBroncos.com, February 2, 2013.

Zaas, Stuart. "Peyton Manning Named FedEx Air Player of the Year." DenverBroncos.com, February 4, 2013.

On the Internet

Manning Foundation
   http://www.peytonmanning.com/
Manning Momentos
   http://www.mountedmemories.com/
Manning Passing Academy
   http://www.manningpassingacademy.com/
Peyton Manning Biography
   http://www.denverbroncos.com/team/roster/Peyton-Manning/5e49338e-cd44-4226-9451-f111c0eb767d

GLOSSARY

cervical fusion—A surgical procedure where bones and discs in the neck are joined together.

competitiveness—The trait of wanting to win, to be the best.

endorsement—An advertisement for companies or organizations made by a celebrity who is paid to promote or sell products or services.

Heisman Trophy—An award given to the best player in college football each year, regardless of position.

herniated disc—A cushiony disc between the bones in the spine or neck that has burst or cracked.

MVP—Most Valuable Player.

NCAA—National Collegiate Athletic Association; the organization that regulates college sports.

nerve—One of the bundles of fibers that communicate information between the brain and the rest of the body.

NFL: National Football League—The organization that regulates professional football in the United States.

NFL Combine—A multi-day camp held each year in February in Indianapolis where the best college football players gather to be tested physically and mentally by NFL teams in preparation for the NFL Draft.

NFL Draft—A multi-day period in April when NFL teams select the best college players.

offensive coordinator—The football coach who runs the offense, makes up the game plan, and calls the plays.

play-action pass—A football play in which the quarterback fakes a handoff to a running back before dropping back to throw a pass.

safety—A play when the offensive team gets tackled—or loses the ball out of bounds—in its own end zone.

SAT: Scholastic Aptitude Test—A test given to high school students to determine their eligibility and readiness for college.

SEC: The Southeastern Conference—A group of southern colleges that compete against one another in a variety of sports.

Sullivan Award—An annual award given to the best amateur athlete in the country based on leadership, character, and athletic ability.